HEALTHY CHOICES

KEEPING SAFE

Cath Senker

PowerKiDS press.

New York

Published in 2008 by The Rosen Publishing Group, Inc.
29 East 21st Street, New York, NY 10010

First Edition

Consultant: Jayne Wright
Design: Sarah Borny

The publishers would like to thank the following for allowing
us to reproduce their pictures in this book:
Getty Images; 8, 13 (bottom) / Hodder Wayland Picture Library; 4, 5, 6, 7,
10, 11, 13 (top), 16, 17, 18, 19, 20, 21 / Zul Mukhida; 9, 14, 15

Library of Congress Cataloging-in-Publication Data

Senker, Cath.
  Keeping safe / Cath Senker. — 1st ed.
     p. cm. — (Healthy choices)
  Includes index.
  ISBN 978-1-4042-4300-2 (library binding)
  1. Safety education—Juvenile literature. I. Title.
  HQ770.7.S46 2008
  363.1071—dc22
                                        2007032791

Manufactured in China

Contents

Why do people have accidents?

However young you are, you can learn to keep safe and help to keep others safe.

Remember that people can have an accident anywhere. Many accidents happen on the roads, because there is so much traffic.

Sometimes children get hurt at school, often in the playground.

One out of every three accidents happens at home.

If someone has hurt themselves, always tell an adult right away. Learn how to use the phone so you can dial 911 for the emergency services if you need to.

If you dialed 911, what would you have to say? (Answer on page 22)

How should I cross the street safely?

Streets are dangerous, because cars go very fast. It is hard for drivers to stop quickly. When you're out of the house, watch out! When you need to cross the street, remember to "Stop, look, listen, and think."

Use *crosswalks* where you can. Wait until the cars stop, or the "Walk" sign lights up, before you cross.

What is this girl doing to make sure she is safe crossing the street?

(Answer on page 23)

In the car, always wear a seatbelt. Never undo it for any reason, until the car has stopped and the driver says you can.

Sometimes drivers can't see people crossing the street. In the winter, it's dark coming home from school or the park. Make sure drivers can see you. Try to wear light-colored clothing. You can put *reflective* bands or stickers on your coat, too.

What do I do if there's a fire?

It's very unlikely that you'll ever be near a fire. Your home will be safer if you have a smoke alarm. If the alarm senses smoke from a fire, it makes a very loud noise.

Make sure you know how to get out of your house quickly and safely in an emergency. If a fire starts, get out as fast as you can. Call 911 from a neighbor's phone.

If a fire starts, in what order should you do these things?

1. **Ask for the fire department**
2. **Call 911**
3. **Get out of the house quickly**
4. **Give your address**

(Answer on page 23)

Ask for the

fire department. When

you are connected, give

your address.

Never play with matches, candles, or

anything else that burns. You could burn

yourself, or even start a fire.

How do I keep safe when I'm out?

When you're out, stay with the older person you're with. Do you know your full name, address, and phone number? Try to learn them in case you ever need to tell someone.

Remember: never go anywhere with a person you don't know.

If you do get lost, call the police. Ask an adult in a store or a parent with children to help you. You can call 911 from a phone booth or a cell phone.

What safety items is this bike rider wearing and why? (Answer on page 23)

If you like to bicycle, scoot, or skate, get ahead—get a helmet! A helmet protects your head. If you fall off, it can save you from a bad injury.

Why should I learn to swim?

It could save your life. If you fall in the water by accident, it will be easier for you to save yourself.

Be careful by rivers, ponds, and lakes. Stand away from the edge. It could be muddy and slippery, and you might fall in. Stay safe and sound—keep your feet on the ground.

In the sea, there are strong **currents**. They can pull you out to sea when you are swimming. Always go in the sea with an adult. Stay and play where you can stand up,even if you know how to swim.

What are the children in both these pictures doing to keep safe? (Answer on page 23)

Do I really need sunscreen?

Yes, you do! It's fun to play in the Sun. A little sunshine does you good. The Sun's rays are very strong, though. They can burn your skin. The Sun is strongest around noon.

Stay cool in the shade during the hottest part of the day.

If you have blonde or red hair and pale skin, you have a high risk of sunburn.

If you don't want to burn, use sunscreen
with at least **SPF** 30 protection.
Cover your shoulders
and thighs.

Remember
that hat!
It protects your
head and your face
from the Sun's rays.
If you burn, it really hurts!
It harms your skin, too.

How do we make food safe to eat?

Make sure you wash your hands before you eat, so you don't get dirt and germs on your food.

Raw foods, such as salad vegetables, often have dirt and germs on them. They may have been sprayed with chemicals to help them grow. Be sure to wash them before you start munching. Then they will be safe for you to enjoy.

Keep fresh foods in the fridge, so they do not turn bad quickly. Food that is rotten can make you sick.

It's fun to eat with friends, but touching other people's food is rude! Sharing food can mean sharing germs, too. Keep pets away from your food, because they carry germs. Don't let the dog get your dinner!

I've cut myself. What do I do?

Ouch! If you cut or scratch yourself badly, blood comes out. If this happens, tell an adult. The adult will need to wash the cut.

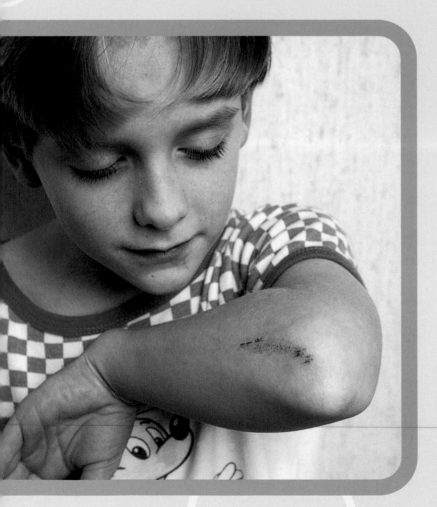

If it is a big cut, you might need some **antiseptic** spray or lotion. Stop the bleeding and keep it clean with a bandage. This will help it to heal faster.

If it's a really deep cut, you may need to go to the hospital. The wound can be stitched or glued by a nurse or a doctor.

You can't put a bandage on a bruise. The bleeding is under the skin, so it won't help. The bruise will heal by itself.

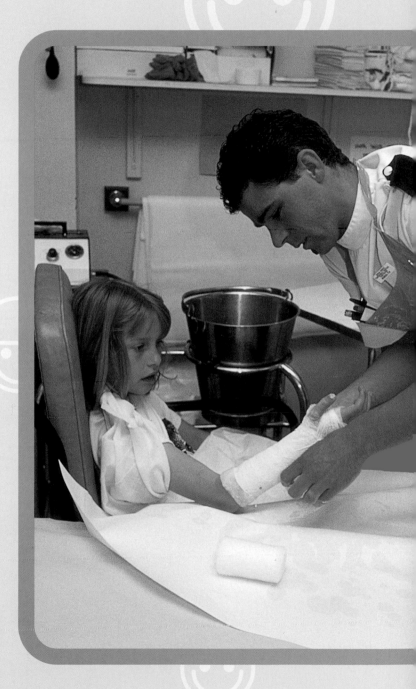

How do I keep safe in the kitchen?

If you're helping in the kitchen, keep your fingers away from sharp knives and machines such as **food processors**.

There are a lot of hot things in the kitchen. Be very careful if you're stirring food on the stove. Keep away from the hot oven and the steaming kettle.

When you use sharp knives, keep your fingers out of the way and always use a cutting board.

Burns are really painful. If you burn yourself, go to the sink and run cold water over the sore part. Tell an adult right away. Keep the water running for 15 minutes—that's a long time! If you're out of the house and there's no faucet, put the burned part in cold water or milk.

Glossary and index

Answers to questions:

P.5 When you call 911, you need to say which service you want. In this case, you need to ask for an ambulance. You will then be connected to the ambulance service. The person you talk to will need to know your name, address, and phone number, and what the problem is.

P.6 To make sure she is safe crossing the street, the girl is holding her babysitter's hand, standing away from the edge of the curb, and looking left and right to see if there is any traffic coming.

P.9 If a fire starts, you should do these things:

1 Get out of the house quickly

2 Call 911

3 Ask for the fire department

4 Give them your address

P.11 The bike rider is wearing a helmet to protect her head and reflective bands so that car drivers can see her clearly.

P.13 The girl by the waterfall is standing back from the edge and is close to an adult. The girl in the sea is staying in shallow water, and she is wearing armbands to help her float.

Finding out more

Books to read:

A First Look at Safety

by Pat Thomas (Barron's Educational, 2003)

Hygiene (What About Health?)

by Cath Senker (Hodder Wayland, 2004)

A Kid's Guide to Staying Safe at Playgrounds: Staying Safe Around Fire: Staying Safe Around Water

all by Maribeth Boelts (PowerKids Press, 1997)

A Kid's Guide to Staying Safe on Bikes

by Maribeth Boelts (PowerKids Press, 1998)

Kids to the Rescue! First Aid Techniques for Kids

by Maribeth Boelts (Parenting Press, 2003)

The Safety Book for Active Kids; Teaching Your Child How to Avoid Everyday Dangers

by Linda Schwartz (Learning Works, 1995)

Web Sites

Due to the changing nature of Internet links, PowerKids Press has developed an online list of Web sites related to the subject of this book. This site is regularly updated. Please use this link to access this list: www.powerkidslinks.com/health/safe